T0388810

Rhinoceros

Written by Alex Hall

Enslow PUBLISHING

From Head to Hoof

Published in 2025 by Enslow Publishing, LLC
2544 Clinton Street
Buffalo, NY 14224

© 2024 BookLife Publishing Ltd.

Written by:
Alex Hall

Edited by:
Rebecca Phillips-Bartlett

Designed by:
Jasmine Pointer

Cataloging-in-Publication Data
Names: Hall, Alex.
Title: Rhinoceros / Alex Hall.
Description: Buffalo, NY : Enslow Publishing, 2025. | Series: From head to hoof | Includes glossary.
Identifiers: ISBN 9781978542013 (pbk.) | ISBN 9781978542020 (library bound) | ISBN 9781978542037 (ebook)
Subjects: LCSH: Rhinoceroses--Juvenile literature. | Rhinoceroses--Behavior--Juvenile literature.
Classification: LCC QL737.U63 H355 2025 | DDC 599.66'8--dc23

Manufactured in the United States of America

CPSIA compliance information: Batch #CW25ENS: For further information contact Enslow Publishing LLC at 1-800-398-2504.

Please visit our website, www.enslowpublishing.com. For a free color catalog of all our high-quality books, call toll free 1-800-398-2504 or fax 1-877-980-4454.

Find us on

Image Credits

All images are courtesy of Shutterstock.com. With thanks to Getty Images, Thinkstock Photo and iStockphoto.
Cover – ARTvektor, YummyBuum, meunierd, chatchawin jampapha. Throughout – ARTvektor, jongcreative. 2–3 – jongcreative, David Havel. 4–5 – Vaclav Sebek, JONATHAN PLEDGER. 6–7 – Erni, JONATHAN PLEDGER. 8–9 – jeep2499, Kurit afshen. 10–11 – Johan Swanepoel, Rob Francis, 3owaldi. 12–13 – visa netpakdee, Johan Swanepoel, ilovezion. 14–15 – Ondrej Prosicky, Francois van Heerden, Nachaliti. 16–17 – ChrisRei, Vasin Buaroong. 18–19 – Udo Kieslich, Corrie Barnard. 20–21 – Jurie Maree, Nachaliti. 22–23 – Cathy Withers-Clarke, Travel Stock.

Contents

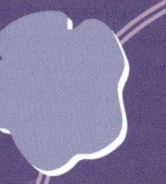

Words that look like <u>this</u> can be found in the glossary on page 24.

Rhinoceros

Rhinoceros are large animals that are known for the horns on their noses. There are five different <u>species</u> of rhinoceros. Rhinoceros live in African grasslands and Asian rainforests.

Rhinoceros are also known as rhinos.

4

The place an animal or plant lives is called its habitat. It is time to find some rhinos in their natural habitat. Let's look at the bodies of some rhinos, from their heads to their hooves.

Head

Rhinos have very heavy heads. White rhinos are the largest rhino species. Their heads can weigh around 992 pounds (450 kg). This is about the same as a small horse.

Rhinos have excellent hearing. Their ears are always moving in different directions. This helps them hear everything that is moving around them. Their ears even move while they are sleeping.

Eyes and Nostrils

Rhinos have small eyes on either side of their head. Rhinos do not have very good eyesight. Rhinos struggle to see a human who is standing more than 55 yards (50 m) away.

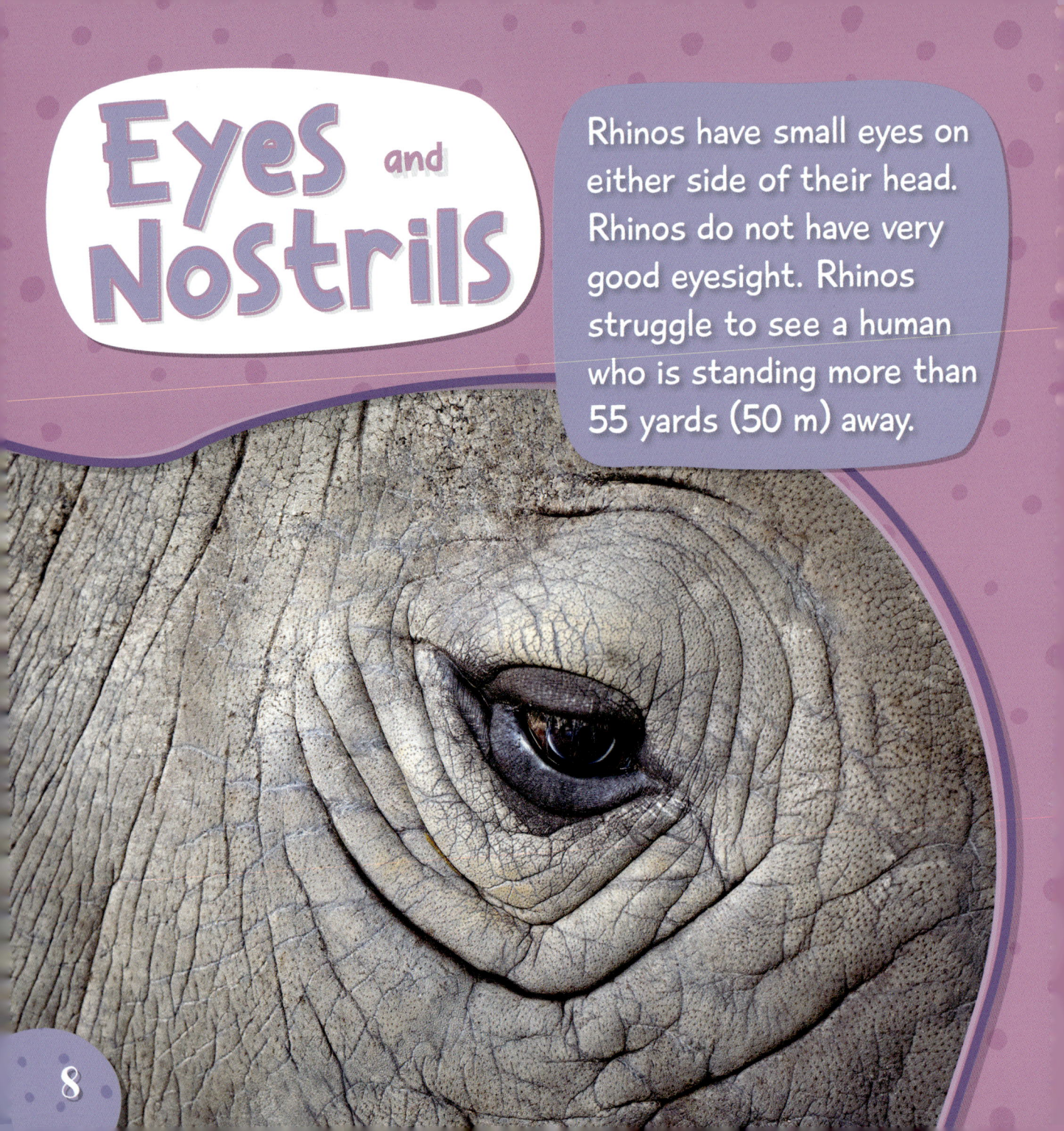

Javan rhino

Rhinos have large nostrils and a good sense of smell. Javan rhinos use their sense of smell to travel through their thick rainforest habitat. Javan rhinos <u>communicate</u> by smelling other rhinos' poo.

9

Mouth

square lip

Different types of rhinos have different shaped lips depending on what they usually eat. White rhinos have square upper lips to eat grass. Black rhinos have pointed lips that help them pick leaves from plants.

All rhinos are herbivores. This means they only eat plants.

pointed lip

10

Rhinos use sounds to communicate. They may snort if they are angry, sneeze if they are scared, or honk if they are relaxed. Sumatran rhinos put lots of sounds together to make songs.

Sumatran rhino

Horn

Rhinoceros are known for the large horns that grow on the front of their faces. In fact, the name rhinoceros actually means "nose horn." Rhinoceros horns can grow to more than 3 feet (1 m) long.

12

Some rhinos use their horns in fights over <u>territory</u>. They also use them to dig for food and water. Some rhino species have two horns. Others only have one horn.

white rhinos

Indian rhino

13

Body

Rhinos are heavy animals. The smallest rhinos weigh around 1,300 pounds (600 kg). The largest can weigh up to 7,700 pounds (3,500 kg). This means some rhinos weigh as much as a large van.

White rhinos are the second largest land <u>mammals</u>.

14

Rhino skin can be over 2 inches (5 cm) thick.

Rhinoceros skin is extremely strong and thick. Their skin protects them from dangerous animals. However, their skin does not protect them from the sun. Rhinos roll in mud to avoid sunburn.

15

Tail

Most of a rhino's tail is not hairy. However, most rhinos have stiff hair at the ends of their tails. The hair on their tails is used to hit bugs that try to bite them.

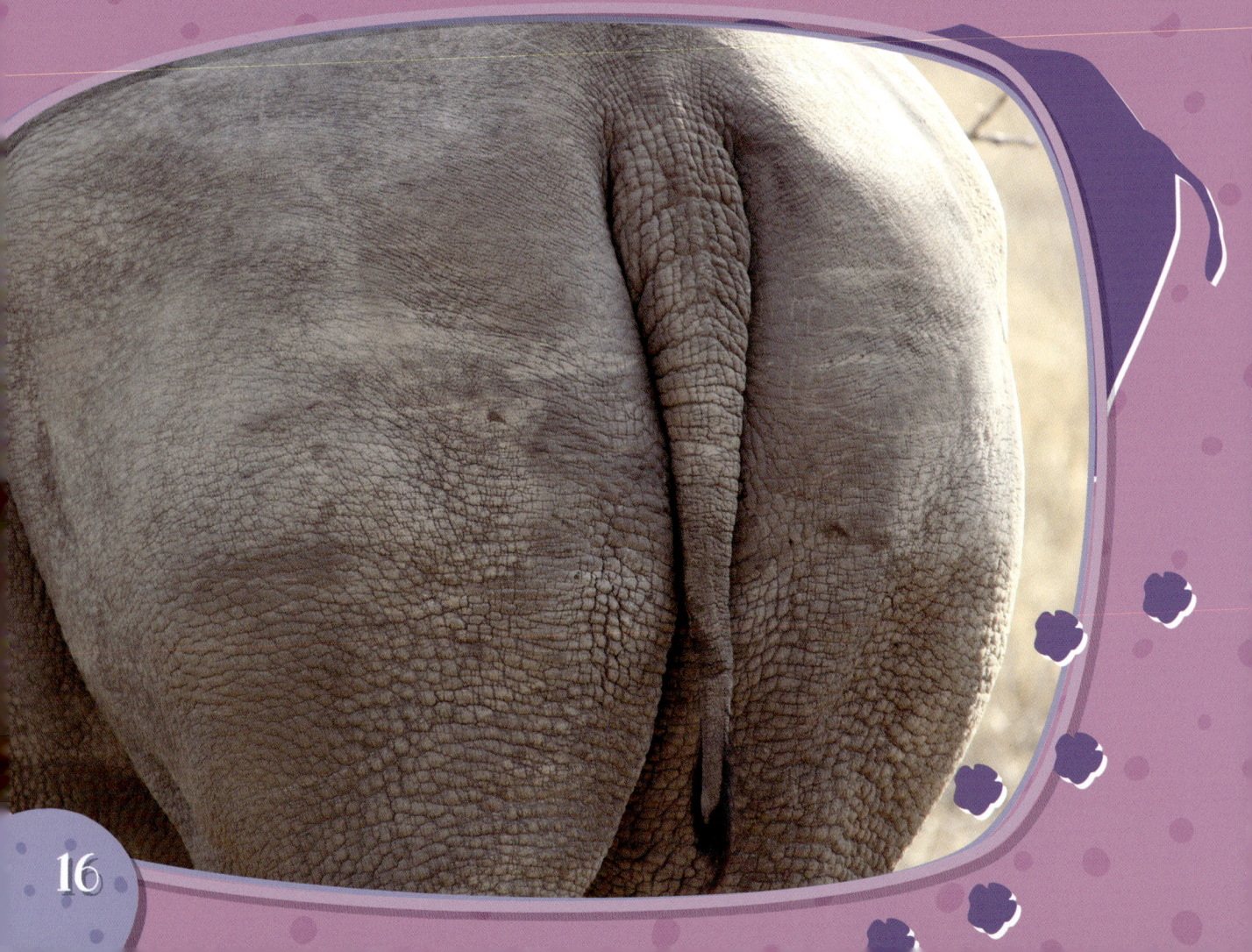

Rhinos also use their tails to show their mood. If a rhino is nervous or scared, it may curl its tail up. Some rhinos use their tails to spread their poo around.

Legs

For such large animals, rhinos' legs are quite short.
Even with short legs, rhinos can run at speeds of
around 31 miles (50 km) an hour. This is faster than
any human has ever run.

18

If a rhino thinks it is in danger, it will charge. Charging is when a rhino runs at something. A rhino may also charge at other rhinos to show that it is the stronger rhino.

Rhinos sometimes charge for no reason because of their bad eyesight.

19

Hooves

Rhinos have three large toes. Each one is covered by a hoof. A rhino's hooves keep growing throughout its whole life. Hooves are made of keratin. Human hair and nails are also made of keratin.

Animals with hooves are known as ungulates.

20

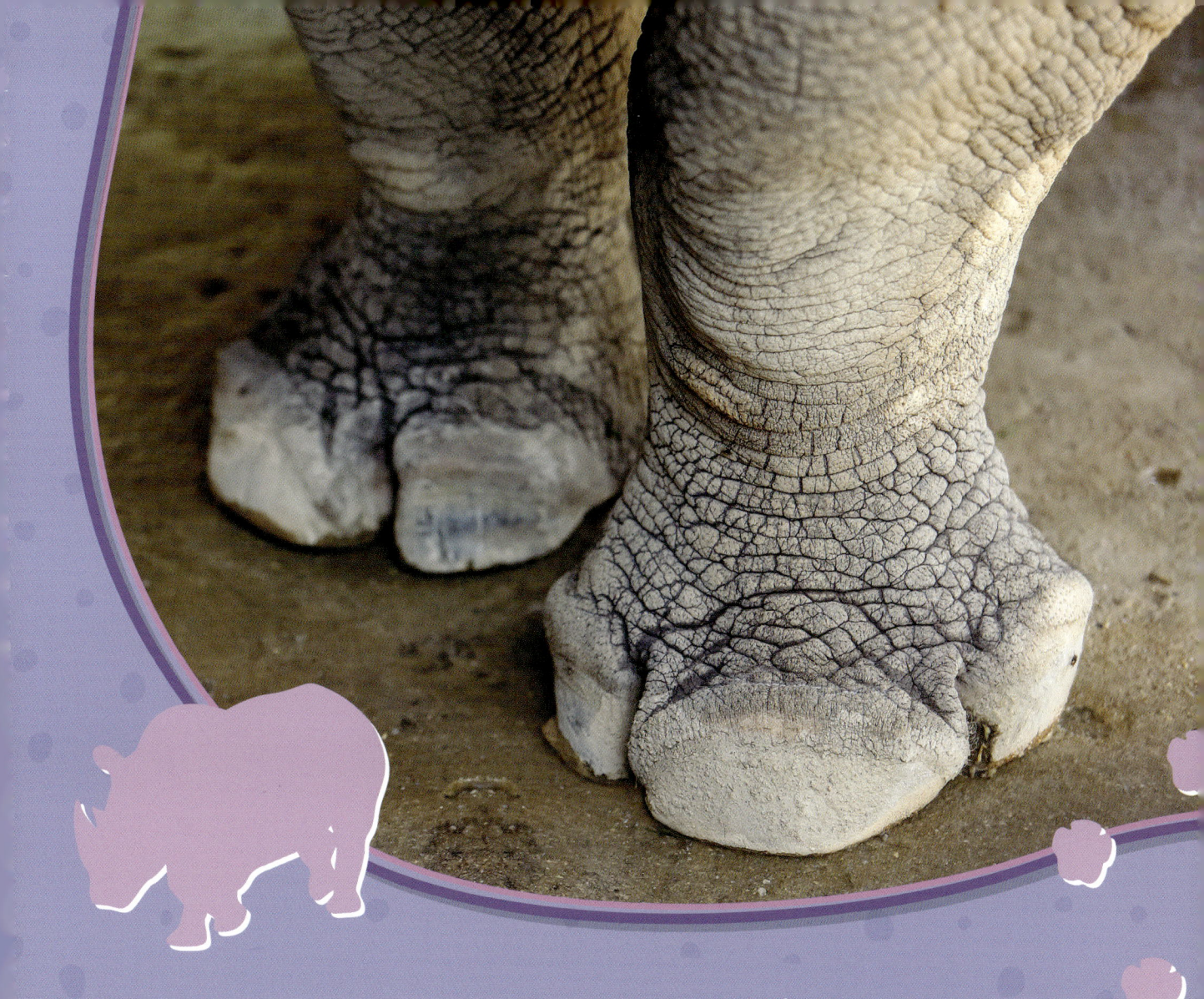

Like all hooved animals, rhinos run on their toes. Rhinos also use their hooves to spread out their weight so that they do not fall over. Their hooves protect their toes from the rough ground.

Life Cycle

Rhinos usually only have one baby rhino at a time. Most rhinos only have a baby every two to four years. Baby rhinos are called calves. Some rhino calves are heavier than some humans.

Life cycles are the changes living things go through during their lives, leading up to being able to have their own young.

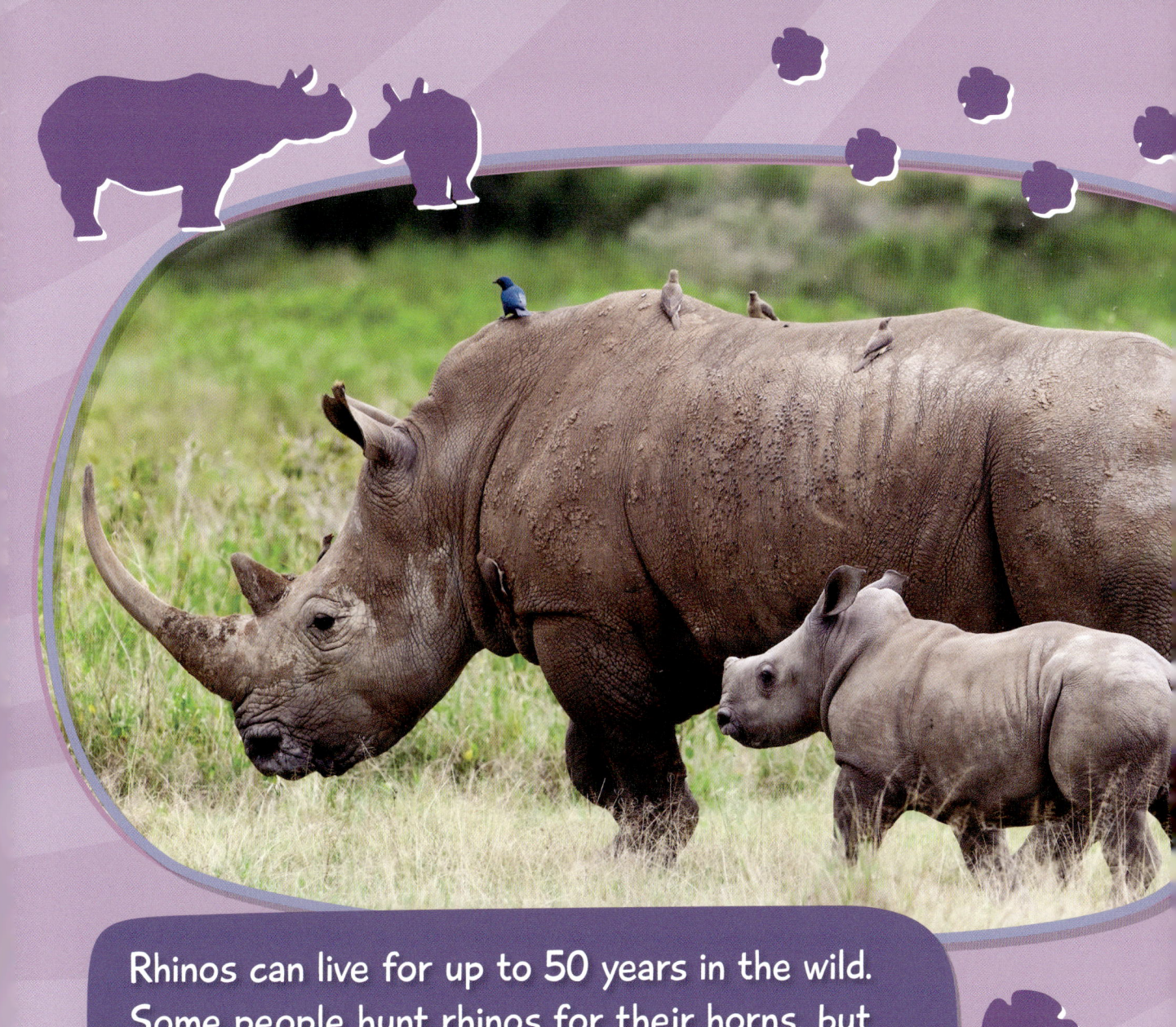

Rhinos can live for up to 50 years in the wild. Some people hunt rhinos for their horns, but it is not allowed. Some rhinos have become <u>endangered</u> because of hunting and <u>habitat loss</u>.

Glossary

Index